THE SOLDIER'S POCKET COMPANION

1746

The Naval & Military Press Ltd

published in association with

Published by
The Naval & Military Press Ltd
Unit 10 Ridgewood Industrial Park,
Uckfield, East Sussex,
TN22 5QE England
Tel: +44 (0) 1825 749494
Fax: +44 (0) 1825 765701
www.naval-military-press.com

in association with

In reprinting in facsimile from the original, any imperfections are inevitably reproduced and the quality may fall short of modern type and cartographic standards.

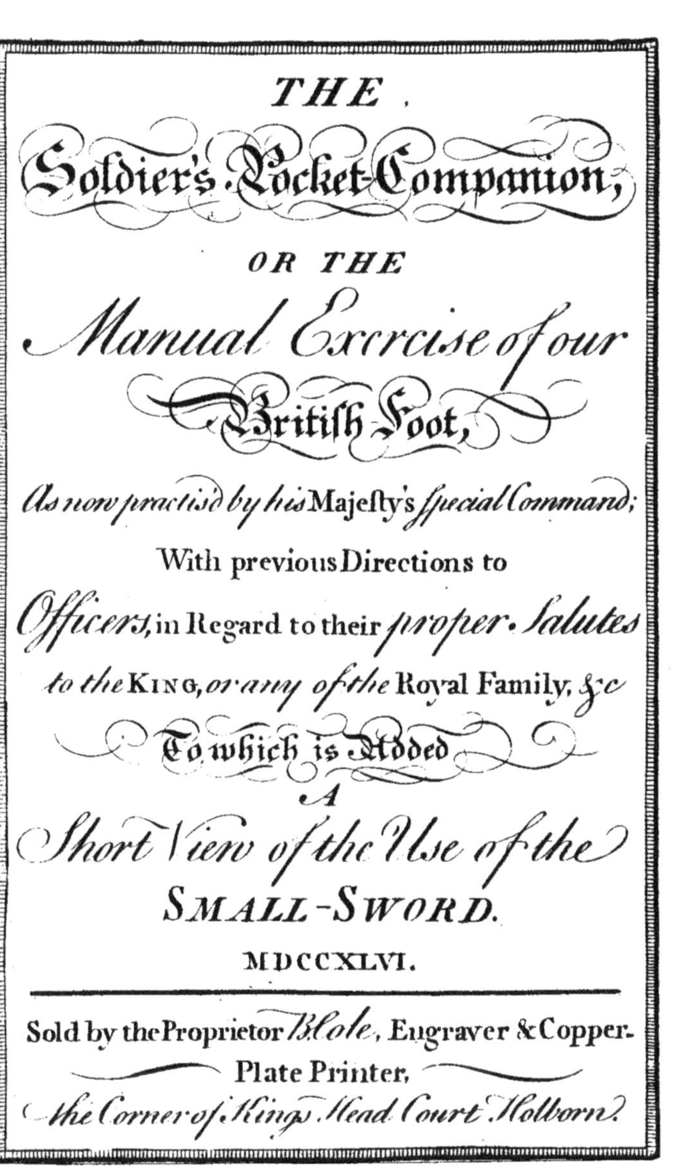

THE Soldier's Pocket-Companion, OR THE Manual Exercise of our British Foot,

As now practis'd by his Majesty's special Command;
With previous Directions to
Officers, in Regard to their proper Salutes
to the KING, or any of the Royal Family, &c

To which is Added
A
Short View of the Use of the
SMALL-SWORD.

MDCCXLVI.

Sold by the Proprietor B. Cole, Engraver & Copper-
Plate Printer,
the Corner of Kings Head Court Holborn.

To the Honourable

Sr. Joseph Hankey, Kt.

Alderman,

And Colonel of the Blue Regiment

Of the CITY of LONDON,

THIS

Manual Exercise of the British Foot

Is with the greatest Respect Dedicated by

Your Honours most Oblig'd,

most Devoted Humble Servt.

Benjamin Cole

The TABLE.

34	Secure your Firelock	3	60 *and* 61
35	Shoulder your Firelock	5	61
36	Poise your Firelock	2	
37	Rest on your Arms	3	62 *to* 64
38	Draw your Bayonet	2	65 *and* 66
39	Fix your Bayonet	5	67 *to* 69
40	Rest your Bayonet	3	70
41	Charge your Bayonet Breast high	4	71 *to* 73
42	Push your Bayonet	2	74
43	Recover your Arms	2	75
44	Rest your Bayonet on your Left Arm	2	76 *and* 77
45	Rest your Bayonet	3	
46	Shoulder your Firelock	4	78
47	Present your Arms	4	
48	To the Right (4 Times)	3	
49	To the Right about	3	79
50	To the Left as you were	3	
51	To the Left (4 Times)	3	
52	To the Left about	3	
53	To the Right as you were	3	84
54	Poise your Firelock	1	
55	Rest on your Arms	3	
56	Unfix your Bayonet	3	85
57	Return your Bayonet	4	86 *and* 87
58	Poise your Firelock	3	87
59	Shoulder your Firelock	4	
	Total Number of Motions	189	

Small Sword.

1	The Guard	88
2	The Thrust in Carte	89
3	The Thrust in Tierce	90
4	The Carte Thrust under the Arm	91
5	The Thrust in Seconde	92
6	Tierce Thrust on Carte Side	93
7	Carte Thrust over the Arm	94
8	The Flanconnade	95
9	The Pass in Tierce	96

I

The Officer muſt ſtand upright and bold, with his Half Pike in his Right Hand, about the ſame Diſtance from his Right Foot as he can extend his Right Arm, holding his Half Pike full in his Right Hand in a direct Line from his Right Shoulder, as far as his Arm will permit without Conſtraint, taking Care that the Half Pike be upright and his Left Hand on his Left Side juſt above the Hip, Thumb behind, Fingers before.

I

The Officer's Salute at ye Head of his Troop.

ATTITUDE. I.

II

ATTITUDE. II .

The Standing Salute.

1ſt Motion.

Fall back with your Right Foot and Hand, and at the ſame Time ſeize your Half Pike with your Left Hand, about two Foot and a half from the Ferrel, keeping both your Arms extended from your Body as far as you can without Conſtraint, and your Aſpect as much as poſſible towards the Front.

The Standing Salute.

2d Motion.

Quit your Right Hand, and at the ſame Time lifting up your Half Pike with your Left Hand, ſeize it again with your Right cloſe to the Ferrel, your Thumb and Fingers extended, your Elbow alſo a little bent and extended; bring up your Right Foot at the ſame Time to the Hollow of the Left or to a *Roman* T) but not too cloſe but ſo as to ſtand firm.

III

ATTITUDE. III.

IV

ATTITUDE. IV.

The Standing Salute.

3d Motion.

Fall back again, with your Right Foot, and lifting up your Elbow, let the Spear of your Half Pike drop within two or three Inches of the Ground; the Staff falling over the Back of the four Fingers of your Left Hand, which muſt be about the Heighth of your Breaſt, with both Arms and Fingers extended.

The Standing Salute.

4th Motion.

Bring up your Right Foot again, near the Hollow of the Left, and at the ſame Time bring your Half Pike to a Recover.

V

ATTITUDE.V.

VI

The Officer's Salute upon a March.

ATTITUDE. I.

The Standing Salute.

5th Motion.

Fall back again with your Right Foot, and at the ſame Time quit your Right Hand, and ſeize your Half Pike as high as you can towards the Spear, that when you come to Order again it may be in a Right Line from your Right Shoulder.

The Standing Salute.

6th Motion.

Quit your Left Hand, and at the ſame Time bring up your Right Hand Pike, and Right Foot together; placing the But End of your Half Pike, and Right Foot, at once on the Ground together, to your proper Front; in a direct Line with your Left Foot, and your Right Arm in a Line from your Right Shoulder, keeping your Pike perpendicular; then ſeize your Hat briſkly with your Left Hand, and bring it down with a briſk Motion by your Side, as low as your Arm will extend.

ATTITUDE II.

ATTITUDE. III.

The Officer muſt March, till he comes within about 20 Paces of the Perſon he is to Salute; with his Half Pike comported as in the Figure.

The Marching Salute.

1ſt Motion.

With a briſk Motion fling off your Right Hand to the Right, with your Half Pike, and turning the Ferrel of your Half Pike foremoſt, bring it on your Right Shoulder, your Right Elbow ſquare, your Left Hand ſet againſt your Left Side, juſt above the Hip, Thumb behind, Fingers before; and the Spear drooping behind, a little lower than the But End.

IX

ATTITUDE. IV.

ATTITUDE V.

The Marching Salute.

2d Motion.

Upon ſtepping forward with your Right Foot, caſt off your Half Pike, in a direct Line from your Shoulder, as far as poſſible without Conſtraint; then ſtepping forward with the Left Foot, at the ſame Time, ſeize your Half Pike, with your Left Hand, within two Foot and a half of the Ferrel.

The Marching Salute.

3d Motion.

Bring up the Right Foot again, opposite to the Hollow of the Left; and at the ſame Time, ſeize your Half Pike, with your Right Hand, at the Ferrel, your Half Pike perpendicularly upright before you, or in a proper Recover.

XI

ATTITUDE .VI .

XII

ATTITUDE. VII.

The Marching Salute.

4th Motion.

Stepping forward with the Left Foot, lift up your Elbow, and let the Spear of your Half Pike drop within two or three Inches of the Ground; the Staff falling over the Back of the four Fingers of the Left Hand, your Body upright, both Arms and Fingers extended.

The Marching Salute.

5th Motion.

Stepping ſorward with your Right Foot, bring it up near the Hollow of the Left; or, to a Roman T: And at the ſame Time, bring up your Half Pike, perpendicularly before you, or to a Recover.

XIII

ATTITUDE. VIII.

XIV

ATTITUDE IX.

The Marching Salute.

6th Motion.

On the next Step with the Left Foot, quit the Ferrel of the Half Pike, with your Right Hand, and ſeize it again with it; about the Middle of the Staff: Fling it off with a ſtraight Arm.

The Marching Salute.

7th Motion.

Stepping forward with the Right Foot, bring it to your Right Shoulder: keeping your Right Elbow ſquare Take off your Hat with your Left Hand, and bring it to your Left Side, by a quick Motion.

XV

The Ensign upon a March.

XVI

The Manual Exercise, &c.

TAKE CARE.

Take Care.

As ſoon as the Word of Command is given, you muſt obſerve a profound Silence, and make no Motion either with your Head, Body, Feet or Hands, but ſuch as ſhall be ordered, looking to the Officer who is to give the Word of Command, carrying your Firelock ſtraight on your Shoulder, Barrel up, Muzzle high, preſſing the Guard to your Breaſt, your Feet a Step Diſtance, the Heels in a Line, and your Toes turned out.

N. B. *This ſhews likewiſe the laſt Motion of Shoulder your Firelock, as in the 26th, 35th, 46th, and 59th Words of Command.*

1. *Join your Right Hand to your Firelock.*

Your Firelock being carried in the forementioned Posture upon the Left Shoulder, you must turn it inwards with the Left Hand, the But to be sunk a little, and at once take hold with the Right Hand behind the Lock, both Elbows in an equal Line, but not constrained.

N. B. *This Figure shews the 1st Motion of the 27th, the 33d, and 36th Words of Command; and the Barrel being suppos'd upwards, (as in the last Figure) instead of the Lock: It likewise shews the 2d of the 26th, the 4th of the 35th, the 3d of the 46th, and the 2d of the 59th Words of Command.*

XVII

Join your Right Hand to your Firelock.

XVIII

Poise your Firelock.

2. *Poiſe your Firelock.*

At the Word of Command, with both Hands and a quick Motion bring up the Firelock from your Shoulder, at the ſame Time thruſt it from you with your Right Hand; in doing which, let your Left Hand fall down by your Side, the ſide Plate oppoſite to your Roller, with your Arm a little bended, the Lock turned outwards, and the Thumb inwards, againſt the Face, and your Feet in the ſame Poſture as when ſhoulder'd.

N. B. *This Figure likewiſe ſhews the 2d Motion of the 29th, the 1ſt of the 34th, the 2d of the 35th, the 2d of the 36th, the 3d of the 46th, and the 3d of the 58th Words of Command.*

3. *Join your Left Hand to your Firelock.*

1ſt Motion.

Turn your Firelock the Barrel towards you, at the ſame Time ſeize it with the Left Hand, ſo that the Little Finger touch the Lock; holding your Firelock in both Hands, with your Arms extended as much as poſſible without Conſtraint; tell 1, 2.

N. B. *This Figure likewiſe ſhews the 2d Motion of the 27th and 33d Words of Command.*

XIX

Join your Left Hand to your Firelock.

XX

Rest your Firelock.

3. *Join your Left Hand to your Firelock.*

2d Motion.

With a quick Motion bring your Firelock down, the But oppoſite to the Right Knee, the Muzzle pointing a little forwards, the Stock in the Left Hand, with your Right Thumb on the Cock, the Forefinger before the Trigger, and the other Fingers behind the Guard. At the ſame Time that you bring down your Firelock, you muſt ſtep a little back with your Right Foot, the Toe pointing to the Right; the Right Knee ſtiff, the Left Knee a little bending, and your Body very ſtraight, and face to the Front as much as poſſible.

N. B. *This is the Reſt, when fac'd to the Left*; Fig. 80, *is the Front Reſt*; Fig. 82, *when fac'd to the Right or Left about*; *and* Fig. 84, *when fac'd to the Right*; *which Figures ſhew the 4th Motion of the 27th, the 3d of the 31ſt, the 4th of the 33d, the 3d of the 40th, the 3d of the 45th, the 4th of the 47th, and the 3d of the 49th, 50th, 51ſt, 52d and 53d Words of Command.*

4. *Cock your Firelock.*

1ſt Motion.

Keep your Thumb upon the Cock, and bring up your Firelock with both Hands before you, the Cock, Roller high; at the ſame Time bring up your Right Foot, the Heel within half a Foot of the Hollow of the Left Foot, and the Toe pointing to the Right, the Firelock cloſe to your Breaſt, that you may the eaſier bend the Cock; tell 1, 2.

2d Motion.

Cock, and at the ſame Time thruſt your Firelock from you with both Hands, holding your Thumb upon the Cock, your Fore-Finger before the Trigger, keeping your Arms ſtretch'd out before your Body.

N. B. *This is the Recover when fac'd to the Left*; Fig. 79, *is the Front Recover*; Fig. 81, *when fac'd to the Right or Left about*; *and* Fig. 83, *when fac'd to the Right*; *which Figures ſhew the 2d Motion of the 12th, the 4th of the 21ſt, the 2d of the 40th, the 1ſt of the 41ſt, the 2d of the 43d, the 2d of the 45th, and the 2d and 3d of the 48th, 49th, 50th, 51ſt, 52d and 53d Words of Command.*

XXI

Cock your Firelock & Recover:

XXII

Present

5. *Present.*

In presenting, take away your Thumb from the Cock, and move the Right Foot a little back, the Toe turned to the Right, the Body to the Front, and place the But in the Hollow, between the Right Breast and the Shoulder, keeping the Fore-Finger before the Trigger, but without touching it, and the other three Fingers behind the Guard, the Elbows in an equal Line, the Head straight upwards, the Body upright, but a little press'd forwards against the Firelock, the Left Knee a little bent, and the Right Knee stiff.

6. *Fire.*

As soon as this Word is given, draw the Trigger briskly with the Fore-Finger, and take care to draw the Trigger but once.

7. *Recover your Arms.*

Bring up your Firelock straight before your Cock, Roller high; the Right Heel near the Hollow of your Left Foot, keeping the Posture as in Explanation, and *Fig.* 21.

8. *Half Cock your Firelock.*

1st Motion.

Bring the Firelock close to your Breast, and half bend the Cock; tell 1, 2.

2d Motion.

Thrust it from you with both Hands, as *Fig.* 21.

9. *Handle your Primer.*

1ſt Motion.

Fall back briſkly with your Right Foot behind the Left, that the Heels come ſtraight behind one another, the Left Toe pointing to the Front; and bring down your Firelock to the Right at the ſame Time with both Hands, and a quick Motion, keeping the Muzzle on a Level with the reſt of the Barrel; tell 1, 2.

N. B. *This Figure ſhews likewiſe the 3d Motion of Shutting the Pan.*

XXIII

Handle your Primers.

1.st Motion.

XXIIII

Handle your Primers.

II^{d}. Motion.

9. *Handle your Primer.*

2d Motion.

Quitting the Firelock with the Right Hand clap your Pouch, and take hold of your Primer, the Thumb on the Spring Cover; tell 1, 2.

N. B. *This Figure likewise shews the 2d Motion of Prime.*

9. *Handle your Primer.*

3d Motion.

Bring it within two Fingers Breadth of the Pan, the Thumb upwards.

XXV

Handle your Primers.

III.[d] Motion.

XXVI

Prime

1.st Motion.

10. *Prime.*

1ſt Motion.

Hold your Firelock ſtill, and turning up that Hand with the Primer, ſhake out as much Powder in the Pan as is neceſſary; let fall your Primer, and open your Hand; tell 1, 2.

2d Motion.

Throw it back behind the But End, the Palm outwards, and remain in that Poſture till the following Word of Command.

11. *Shut your Pan.*

1ſt Motion.

Take hold of the Steel with your Thumb upwards, and your two Fore-Fingers under; tell 1, 2.

2d Motion.

Shut your Pan; tell 1, 2.

3d Motion.

Seize your Firelock with your Right Hand behind the Lock; (as in *Fig.* 23.) tell 1, 2.

4th Motion.

Bring up your Firelock to the Recover, as *Figure* 21.

N. B. *If in this Figure the Fingers are ſuppoſed over the Steel of the Pan, it will ſhew the two firſt Motions.*

12. *Cast about to Charge.*

1st Motion.

Turn the Firelock with both Hands, the Barrel outwards; tell 1, 2.

XXVII

Cast about to Charge.

1.st Motion.

XXVIII

Cast about to Charge.

II.[d] Motion.

12. *Cast about to Charge.*

2d Motion.

Let go the Right Hand, bringing down the Firelock with the Left; step forwards with the Right Foot, tho' not directly before the Left; but place it a little to the Right, that the Body may present itself the better forwards; taking hold of the Muzzle with the Right Hand, that the bringing down of the Firelock, the moving of the Right Foot and the taking hold of the Muzzle, be done at the same Time; hold it with your Right Hand, the Thumb upwards near the Rammer, and the Barrel downwards, keeping the Body straight, only the Right Knee a little bent, which must remain so till you have charged.

N. B. *This Figure likewise shews the 1st Motion of the 13th, and the 2d and 3d of the 23d Words of Command.*

13. *Handle your Cartridge.*

1ſt Motion.

Bring the Firelock with both Hands to your Body; tell 1, 2.

2d Motion.

Quit your Firelock with your Right Hand, holding it with your Left Hand in a Ballance, the Muzzle pointing a little forward, and at the ſame Time clap your Pouch, and take hold of your Cartridge; tell 1, 2.

3d Motion.

Bring it within one Inch of the ſide of the Muzzle, the Thumb upwards, and the Right Elbow ſquare.

XXIX

Handle your Cartridge.

II^d Motion.

XXX

Open your Cartridge.

1.st Motion.

14. *Open your Cartridge.*

1ſt Motion.

Bring the Cartridge to your Mouth, and bite off the Top, ſinking your Elbow; tell 1, 2.

2d Motion.

Bring it again to its former Place, holding it with the Thumb upwards.

15. *Charge with Cartridge.*

1ſt Motion.

Bring the Cartridge juſt before the Muzzle, turning up your Hand and Elbow, and fix it in at the ſame Time; tell 1, 2.

2d Motion.

Raiſe your two Fore-Fingers; tell 1, 2.

3d Motion.

Clap them on the Muzzle briſkly, and remain ſo with the Elbow ſquare.

16. *Draw your Rammer.*

1st Motion.

Seize the Rammer with your Fore-Finger and Thumb of your Right Hand, the Thumb upwards; tell 1, 2.

XXXI

Draw your Rammer.

1.st Motion.

XXXII

Draw your Rammer.

II.[d] Motion.

16. *Draw your Rammer.*

2d Motion.

Draw it out as far as your Arm will reach; tell 1, 2.

N. B. *This Figure likewise shews the 1st Motion of Recover your Rammer.*

16. *Draw your Rammer.*

3d Motion.

Take hold of it cloſe to the Stock, turning the Thumb downwards; tell 1, 2.

N. B. *This Figure ſhews likewiſe the 2d Motion of Recovering the Rammer.*

XXXIII

Draw your Rammer.

III.ᵈ Motion.

XXXIV

Draw your Rammer.

IV.th Motion.

16. *Draw your Rammer.*

4th Motion.

Draw it quite out, holding it between the Thumb and the two Fore-Fingers, the whole Arm ſtretch'd out in a Line with the Right Shoulder; the ſmall End towards you, and the other from you in an even Line.

N. B. *This Figure ſhews likewiſe the 3d Motion of Recovering the Rammer.*

17. *Shorten your Rammer.*

1ſt Motion.

Move the middle Finger, which ſupports the Rammer, and turn it quick with the thick End down, and hold it ſo in your Hand, with an out-ſtretch'd Arm, in a Line with your Shoulder, the Thumb upwards; tell 1, 2.

N. B. *This Figure likewiſe ſhews the 1ſt Motion of the 21ſt Word of Command, only the thick End of the Rammer is upwards.*

XXXV

Shorten your Rammer.
1.st Motion.

XXXVI

Shorten your Rammer.

II.^{d} Motion.

17. *Shorten your Rammer.*

2d Motion.

Set the thick End againſt the lower Part of your Breaſt; tell 1, 2.

N. B. *This Figure ſhews likewiſe the 2d Motion of the 21ſt Word of Command.*

17. *Shorten your Rammer.*

3d Motion.

Slip your Hand down to a Hand's Breadth of the End, the Rammer in a Line with the Barrel, the Thumb upwards, and the Elbow a little turn'd out from the Body.

N. B. *This Figure likewiſe ſhews the* 3d *Motion of the* 21*ſt Word of Command.*

XXXVII

Shorten your Rammer

III.^d Motion.

XXXVIII

Put it in the Barrell.

I.st Motion.

18. *Put it in the Barrel.*

1ſt Motion.

Bring the Rammer a little above the Muzzle, and place the thick End on the Cartridge; then tell 1, 2.

N. B. *This Figure likewiſe ſhews the 1ſt Motion of Returning the Rammer, only there the ſmall End is put into the Stock inſtead of the thick End into the Barrel.*

18. *Put it in the Barrel.*

2d Motion.

Thruſt it down as far as your Hand will permit; tell 1, 2.

N. B. *This Figure likewiſe ſhews the 2d Motion of Returning the Rammer, only with the Difference noted in the 1ſt Motion.*

XXXIX

Put it in the Barrell.

II.^d Motion.

XL

Put it in the Barrell.

III^{d} Motion.

18. *Put it in the Barrel.*

3d Motion.

Seize it about the Middle; then tell 1, 2.

N. B. *This Figure likewiſe ſhews the 3d Motion of Returning the Rammer, with the Difference noted in the 1ſt Motion.*

18. *Put it in the Barrel.*

4th Motion.

Thruſt it down as before; tell 1, 2.

N. B. *This Figure likewiſe ſhews the 4th Motion of Returning the Rammer, with the Difference noted in the 1ſt Motion.*

XLI

Put it in the Barrell

IV.th Motion.

XLII

Put it in the Barrell.

V.th Motion.

18. *Put it in the Barrel.*

5th Motion.

Seize it at the Top; tell 1, 2.

N. B. *This Figure likewise ſhews the 5th Motion of Returning the Rammer, only in that the Palm of the Hand is put at the Top of the Rammer.*

18. *Put it in the Barrel.*

6th Motion.

Thruſt it down to your Hand, holding the Rammer faſt with the Thumb upwards.

19. *Ram down your Charge.*

1ſt Motion.

Draw the Rammer as far as the Arm unforc'd will permit; tell 1, 2.

N. B. *Fig.* 42. *ſhews this Motion.*

2d Motion.

Ram down the Charge with an ordinary Force, hold the Rammer as before.

N. B. *This Fig. ſhews this Motion.*

20. *Recover your Rammer.*

1ſt Motion.

Draw your Rammer with a quick Motion till Half of it be out of the Barrel; (as *Fig.* 32.) tell 1, 2.

2d Motion.

Seize it cloſe to the Muzzle with the Thumb downwards; (as *Fig.* 33.) tell 1, 2.

3d Motion.

Draw it quite out of the Barrel, holding it with the Thick End towards your Shoulder, obſerving the ſame Poſition, as in Explanation and *Fig.* 34.

21. *Shorten your Rammer.*

1ſt Motion.

Turn down the ſmall End of the Rammer with your two Fore Fingers and Thumb; (as *Fig.*35.) tell 1, 2.

2d Motion.

Set it againſt your Breaſt; (as *Fig.* 36.) tell 1, 2.

3d Motion.

Slip your Hand within a Foot of the End; as *Fig.*37.

XLIII

Put it in the Barrell.
VIth Motion.

XLIV

Cast off your Firelock

1.st Motion.

22. *Return your Rammer.*

1ſt Motion.

Bring the ſmall End with a gentle Turn under the Barrel, and place it in the Stock; (as *Fig.* and *Note* 38.) tell 1, 2.

2d Motion.

Thruſt it in as far as your Hand will permit; (as *Fig.* 39.) tell 1, 2.

3d Motion.

Seize it in the Middle; (as *Fig.* 40.) tell 1, 2.

4th Motion.

Thruſt it down as before; as *Fig.* 41. tell 1, 2.

5th Motion.

Set the Palm of your Hand againſt the thick End; (as *Fig.* and *Note* 42.) tell 1, 2.

6th Motion.

Thruſt it quite down.

23. *Caſt off your Firelock.*

1ſt Motion.

Extend your Right Arm to the Right, in a Line with your Shoulder; tell 1, 2.

2d Motion.

Take hold of your Firelock, your Thumb even with the Muzzle: as *Fig.* 28. tell 1, 2.

3d Motion.

Thruſt your Firelock from your Body; as Explanation and *Fig.* 28.

24. *Your Right Hand under the Lock.*

Face on the Left Heel to the Left, at the ſame Time turning the Muzzle directly up, you ſeize the Firelock with the Right Hand behind the Lock, holding the Firelock from your Body, and your Hands as low as you can without Conſtraint.

25. *Poiſe your Firelock.*

Face very quick on the Left Heel to the Right, and at the ſame Time bring the Firelock with the Right Hand before you, letting your Left Hand fall down by your Side, puſhing the Firelock ſuddenly with the Right Hand forwards, the Arm a little bended, ſo that the thruſting forwards of the Firelock, and the ſetting down of the Right Foot, be done at the ſame Time; as *Fig.* 18.

XLV

Your Right Hand under the Lock.

XLVI

Shoulder your Firelock.

1st Motion.

26. *Shoulder your Firelock.*

1ſt Motion.

Turn your Firelock with the Right Hand, the Barrel outwards, and the Guard inwards, againſt the Left Shoulder; at the ſame Time ſeize the But with your Left Hand, placing your Thumb in the Hollow; tell 1, 2.

2d Motion.

Bring it with both Hands upon the Left Shoulder without moving your Head, and keep both Elbows in a Line; (as *Fig.* and *Note* 17.) tell 1, 2.

3d Motion.

Quit your Right Hand, letting it fall down by your Side, ſinking your Left Elbow at the ſame Time; (as *Fig.* 16.)

27. *Reſt your Firelock.*

1ſt Motion.

Join your Right Hand; as in Explanation and *Fig.* 17.

2d Motion.

Come to your Poiſe; as in Explanation and *Fig.* 18.

3d Motion.

Seize your Firelock with your Left Hand; as in Explanation and *Fig.* 19.

4th Motion.

Come down to your Reſt; as in Explanat. and *Fig.* 20.

28. *Order your Firelock.*

1ſt Motion.

Slip up your Left Hand as high as your Right Shoulder; bring back at the ſame Time your Right Hand towards your Right Thigh, holding your Firelock perpendicular; tell 1, 2.

XLVII

Order your Firelock.

1.st Motion.

XLVIII

Order your Firelock.

II.^{d} Motion.

28. *Order your Firelock.*

2d Motion.

Let go the Right Hand, ſinking the Firelock with the Left; at the ſame Time ſeize your Firelock with the Right Hand near the Muzzle, that the Thumb be upwards and even with it; tell 1, 2.

28. *Order your Firelock.*

3d Motion.

Quit your Left Hand, and ſit down the But End of the Firelock upon the Ground even with your Toe, at the Outſide of your Right Foot, and perform it with that Quickneſs, that your Right Foot and the Firelock come down at the ſame Time, the Heels in a ſtraight Line, the Toes turned outwards, letting your Right Arm hang from the Hand to the Elbow by the Side of the Firelock, and the Left Hand hanging by the Left Side.

N. B. *This Figure likewiſe ſhews the 4th Motion of Taking up the Firelock.*

XLIX

Order your Firelock.

III.d Motion.

L

Ground your Firelock

1.st Motion.

29. *Ground your Firelock.*

1ſt Motion.

Lift up your Right Foot, and making a half Face to the Right, place it againſt the flat End of the But, and at the ſame Time turn the Barrel of your Firelock towards your Body; tell 1, 2.

29. *Ground your Firelock.*

2d Motion.

Step directly forward with the Left Foot, slipping your Right Hand to the Middle of the Barrel, your Left Hand hanging down, and at the same Time you bring down your Right Knee on the Firelock, looking up; tell 1, 2.

N. B. *This Figure shews likewise the 2d Motion of Taking up the Firelock.*

Ground your Firelock.
II.[d] Motion.

Ground your Firelock.
III.[d] Motion.

29. *Ground your Firelcck.*

3d Motion.

Raiſe your Self again, ſtepping back with your Left Foot, and keeping your Body half fac'd to the Right; tell 1, 2.

N. B. *This Figure ſhews likewiſe the 1ſt Motion of Taking up the Firelock.*

29. *Ground your Firelock.*

4th Motion.

Turn your Right Foot on the Heel over the But End, and bring in your Body to its proper Front, letting both Arms hang down by your Sides.

30. *Take up your Firelock.*

1ſt Motion.

Turn your Right Foot on your Heel over the But End of the Firelock, and ſet it down behind the ſame, making a half Face to the Right; extend your Right Arm a little to your Right Side; (as *Fig.* 52.) tell 1, 2.

2d Motion.

Step forward with the Left Foot along the Firelock; at the ſame Time take hold of it by the Middle of the Barrel with an out-ſtretch'd Arm and a ſtiff Body; (as *Fig.* 51.) tell 1, 2.

3d Motion.

Raiſe up yourſelf and the Firelock again; bringing back the Left Foot; then tell 1, 2.

4th Motion.

Lift up your Right Foot again and ſet it at the Inſide of the But, ſlipping up your Right Hand as high as the Muzzle, and turning the Barrel towards the Right Shoulder; ſtand in the Poſture that is ſhewn in Explanation and *Fig.* 49.

N. B. *You muſt obſerve in Grounding your Firelock not to keep your Hand on the Muzzle, but to ſink them to the Middle of the Barrel; and in taking it up, to take hold at the ſame Place, then alſo ſlip your Hand up to the Muzzle with Eaſe.*

Note, *It is further to be obſerv'd, that at the Grounding, and Taking up your Firelock, you muſt keep up your Head.*

Ground your Firelock.
IV.th Motion.

LIV

Rest your Firelock.
1.st Motion.

31. *Rest your Firelock.*

1st Motion.

Turn your Thumb inwards, and slip your Hand as low as the Arm will permit without Constraint; tell 1, 2.

31. *Rest your Firelock.*

2d Motion.

Raiſe your Firelock with the Right Hand, taking hold of it at the ſame Time with the Left, juſt under the Right; tell 1, 2.

3d Motion.

Let go your Right Hand, and place it behind the Lock, ſtepping back with your Right Foot at the ſame Time, ſo that the reſting your Firelock, and ſtepping back with the Right Foot, be done at once; then keep your Firelock, Body, and Feet in the ſame Poſture, as in Explanation and *Fig.* 20.

LV

Rest your Firelock.

II.^{d} Motion.

LVI

Club your Firelock.

1.st Motion.

32. *Club your Firelock.*

1ſt Motion.

Keep your Firelock firm in your Left Hand, and caſt it about with your Right; bring up the Right Foot at the ſame Time, and take hold of it with the Right Hand as low as you can without Conſtraint, the Guard right againſt your Eyes, the Muzzle and Left Thumb downwards, and the Lock from you; tell 1, 2.

N. B. *This Figure likewiſe ſhews the 3d Motion of the Return from the Club to the Reſt, only then the Barrel is from you.*

32. *Club your Firelock.*

2d Motion.

Let go the Left Hand, and place it at the End of the Stock, raiſing the Firelock at the ſame Time with the Right Hand, and keeping it with out-ſtretch'd Arms oppoſite to the Left Shoulder; tell 1, 2.

N. B. *This Figure likewiſe ſhews the 2d Motion of returning from the Club to the Reſt, only the Barrel from you inſtead of the Lock.*

LVII

Club your Firelock.

II.^d Motion.

LVIII

Club your Firelock.

III.ᵈ Motion.

32. *Club your Firelock.*

3d Motion.

Bring it on the Left Shoulder with the Lock upwards; tell 1, 2.

N. B. *This Figure likewise shews the 1st Motion of the Return from the Club to the Rest; only there the Barrel is upwards instead of the Lock.*

32. *Club your Firelock.*

4th Motion.

Quit your Right Hand with a quick Motion, and let it hang down by your Right Side.

33. *Reſt your Firelock.*

1ſt Motion.

Turn your Firelock with the Left Hand inwards ſinking your Firelock, and at the ſame Time take hold with your Right Hand a Handful above the Left, the Elbows in an Equal Line; (ſee *Fig.* and *Note* 58.) tell 1, 2.

2d Motion.

Bring it with both Hands before your Body, the But high, and your Arms extended; (ſee *Fig.* and *Note* 57.) tell 1, 2.

3d Motion.

Let go your Left Hand, and ſink your Firelock with the Right, let the Guard be even with your Eyes, ſeizing it at the ſame Time, near the Lock, with your Left Hand turned, the Thumb downwards; (ſee *Fig.* and *Note* 56.) tell 1, 2.

4th Motion.

Let go your Right Hand, and turn the Firelock with the Left, bringing the But End down, and come to your Reſt, ſtepping back with your Right Foot; as Explanation and *Fig.* 20.

LIX

Club your Firelock.

IV.th Motion.

LX

Secure your Firelock.
II.^d Motion.

34. *Secure your Firelock.*

1ſt Motion.

Come briſkly to your Poiſe, (as *Fig.* 18) tell 1, 2.

2d Motion.

Seize the Firelock with your Left Hand a Handful from the Lock, turning the Barrel outwards, and bringing the Firelock oppoſite to your Left Shoulder, the Muzzle directly up; tell 1, 2.

N. B. *The 1ſt Motion in returning from the Secure to the Shoulder, differs from this, in being brought cloſe to the Body, and the Lock outwards.*

34. *Secure your Firelock.*

3d Motion.

Quit your Right Hand, and bring the Firelock with the Left Hand under your Left Arm, the Lock betwixt the Wrist and the Elbow, the Barrel downwards, and the Muzzle a Foot from the Ground.

35. *Shoulder your Firelock.*

1st Motion.

Bring the Firelock with a quick Motion before you, the Muzzle upwards, and the Lock turn'd outwards, and seize it at the same Time with the Right Hand under the Lock; (see *Fig.* and *Note* 60.) tell 1, 2.

2d Motion.

Thrust it from you with the Right Hand, and let go the Left, at the same Time come to your Poise; (as *Fig.* 18.) tell 1, 2.

3d Motion.

Clap your Left Hand to the But, the Thumb in the Hollow; (as Expla. and *Fig.*46.) tell 1,2.

4th Motion.

Lay it on your Shoulder; as Expla.46. tell 1, 2.

5th Motion.

Quit your Right Hand; as in Explan. 46. and *Fig.* 16.

36. *Poise your Firelock.*

This is done as in Explanat. and *Fig.* 17, 18.

LXI

Secure your Firelock.
III.[d] Motion.

LXII

Rest on your Arms.
1.st Motion.

37. *Reſt on your Arms.*

1ſt Motion.

Sink your Firelock as low as you can without Conſtraint with your Right Hand, ſeizing it at the ſame Time with your Left, the Height of your Chin, the Left Elbow turn'd out; tell 1, 2.

37. *Rest on your Arms.*

2d Motion.

Seize the Muzzle with your Right Hand, tell 1, 2.

LXIII

Rest on your Arms.

II.d Motion.

LXIV

Rest your Arms
III.d Motion.

37. *Reſt on your Arms.*

3d Motion.

Bring the But to the Ground, ſlipping up your Left Hand at the ſame Time, cloſe to your Right.

38. *Draw your Bayonet.*

1ſt Motion.

Seize your Bayonet with the Right Hand, the Thumb in Hollow; tell 1, 2.

LXV

Draw your Bayonet.
1.st Motion.

LXVI

Draw your Bayonet.

II^{d} Motion.

38. *Draw your Bayonet.*

2d Motion.

Draw it out briſkly, facing full to the Right, with an extended Arm, the Point of the Bayonet ſtraight up, with your Thumb in the Hollow of the Shank, that the Notch of the Socket may come even with the Sight of the Barrel, when you fix it on the Muzzle.

39. *Fix your Bayonet.*

1ſt Motion.

Turn briſkly up with Foot and Hand to the proper Front, placing the Socket of the Bayonet on the Muzzle; tell 1, 2.

2d Motion.

Thruſt it down as far as the Notch will permit; tell 1, 2.

LXVII

Fix your Bayonet.
1.st Motion.

LXVIII

Fix your Bayonet.
III.^{d} Motion.

39. *Fix your Bayonet.*

3d Motion.

Turn it from you, and fix it; tell 1, 2.

39. *Fix your Bayonet.*

4th Motion.

Caſt your Hand a little to the Right, with a ſquare Elbow; tell 1, 2.

5th Motion.

Seize your Firelock with the Palm of your Right Hand on the Back of your Left, as *Fig.* 64.

LXIX

Fix your Bayonet
IV.th Motion.

LXX

Rest your Bayonet.
1.st Motion.

40. *Reſt your Bayonet.*

1ſt Motion.

Raiſe the Firelock with your Right Hand as high as your Forehead, and ſlip your Left Hand at the ſame Time as low as poſſible without Conſtraint; tell 1, 2.

2d Motion.

Raiſe your Firelock with your Left Hand, turning the Barrel towards you; and at the ſame Time ſeize it under the Lock, obſerving the Poſture as Explanation, and *Fig.* 21. tell 1, 2.

3d Motion.

Then come to your Reſt, as Explanation, and *Fig.* 20.

41. *Charge your Bayonet Breaſt high.*

1ſt Motion.

Bring your Firelock to the Recover; as *Fig.* 21. tell 1, 2.

2d Motion.

Throw back your Right Hand; tell 1, 2.

LXXI

Charge your Bayonet Breast high.
II.ᵈ Motion.

LXXII

Charge yʳ Bayonet Breast High.
IIIᵈ. Motion.

41. *Charge your Bayonet Breaſt high.*

3d Motion.

Clap the Palm againſt the Plate of the But, the Barrel being towards you; tell 1, 2.

41. *Charge your Bayonet Breaſt high.*

4th Motion.

Fall back with your Right Foot, your Heels in a Line; come to your Charge, having the But End in a full Right Hand, your Thumb upon it, the Barrel upwards, the Left Elbow turned out from the Body, and the Point of the Bayonet the Height of your Breaſt.

LXXIII

Charge y^r Bayonet Breast High.
IVth Motion.

LXXIV

Push your Bayonet.
1.st Motion.

42. *Push your Bayonet.*

1st Motion.

Push your Bayonet forwards, without raising or sinking the Point; and at the same Time bring the But of the Firelock before your Left Breast; tell 1, 2.

2d Motion.

Bring it back to its former Posture.

43. *Recover your Arms.*

1ſt Motion.

Seize your Firelock with the Right Hand behind the Cock; tell 1, 2.

2d Motion.

Come up to your Recover.

LXXV

Recover your Arms.

1st Motion.

LXXVI

Rest ye Bayonet on your left Arm.
1st Motion.

44. *Rest your Bayonet on your Left Arm.*

1st Motion.

Turn the Lock of the Firelock from you; tell 1, 2.

44. *Reſt your Bayonet on your Left Arm.*

2d Motion.

Stepping out with the Right Foot let go your Left Hand, ſink your Fire-lock, and at the ſame Time take hold of the Cock and Steel with your Left Hand, the Cock lying on your middle Finger, and the lower Joint of your Thumb on the Steel; keep both Arms as low as poſſible without Conſtraint; the But between your Thighs, and the Bayonet pointing exactly to your Left, and as far from your Shoulder, as the Situation of both your Arms and the But will permit.

LXXVII

Rest yr. Bayonet on your left Arm.

IId. Motion.

LXXVIII.

Rest your Bayonet.

1.st Motion.

45. *Rest your Bayonet.*

1st Motion.

Slip your Left Hand without moving the Firelock, and take hold of the Stock above the Lock, your Thumb inwards; tell 1, 2.

2d Motion.

Bring the Firelock to the Recover, with your Right Heel against the Hollow of the Left Foot, as *Fig.* 21. tell 1, 2.

3d Motion.

Come briskly to the Rest.

46. *Shoulder your Firelock.*

1st Motion.

Come briskly to the Poise, as *Fig.* 18.

2d Motion.

Clap your Left Hand on the But, as *Fig.* 46.

3d Motion.

Lay the Firelock on your Shoulder, as *Fig.* 17. and Note.

4th Motion.

Quit your Right Hand, as *Fig.* 16.

47. *Present your Arms.*

This is done as in Explanation 27.

48. *To the Right, To the Right, To the Right, To the Right,*

1ſt Motion.

In each of theſe four Facings you firſt come to the Recover, as *Fig.* 21. tell 1, 2..

2d Motion.

Face upon the Left Heel to the Right, keeping your Firelock well Recover'd; tell 1. 2.

3d Motion.

Come to your Reſt nimbly, ſtepping back with your Right Foot.

49. *To the Right about.*

This is done as in the foregoing Explanation; only you now face to the Right about.

50. *To the Left as you were.*

Obſerve the ſame Time as in the other Facings; coming briſkly to the Left about.

LXXIX

The Recover in Front.

LXXX

The Rest in Front.

LXXXI

The Recover when Fac'd, to the Right or Left about.

LXXXII

The Rest when Fac'd to ye Right or Left about.

LXXXIII

The Recover when Fac'd to the Right.

LXXXIV

The Rest when Fac'd to the Right

51. *To the Left,*
To the Left,
To the Left,
To the Left,

This is perform'd like the Facings to the Right, only with this Difference, that you turn upon the Left Heel to the Left every Time, the fourth Part of a Circle; and obſerve, as in Explanation 48.

52. *To the Left about.*

This is done as in Explanation 50.

53. *To the Right as you were.*

This is done as in Explanation 49.

54. *Poiſe your Firelock.*

Come briſkly to the Poiſe in one Motion.

55. *Reſt on your Arms.*

This is done as in Explanation 37.

56. *Unfix your Bayonet.*

1ſt Motion.

Slip up your Bayonet with the Right Hand; tell 1, 2.

2d Motion.

Turn it towards you; tell 1, 2.

3d Motion.

Slip it quite off the Muzzle, thruſting it from you at the ſame Time.

LXXXV

Unfix your Bayonet.
II.d Motion.

LXXXVI

Return your Bayonet.

II.ᵈ Motion.

57. *Return your Bayonet.*

1ſt Motion.

Turn briſkly to the Right on the Left Heel, with an extended Arm, and the Point of the Bayonet upwards; (as *Fig.* 66.) tell 1, 2.

2d Motion.

Sink the Point of your Bayonet, and place it in the Scabbard; tell 1, 2.

57. *Return your Bayonet.*

3d Motion.

Thruſt it quite in, holding up your Head, and looking to the Right; tell 1. 2.

4th Motion.

Extend your Arm to its former Poſture, and come briſkly up to your proper Front, ſeizing the Firelock near the Muzzle, with your Right Hand above the Left.

58. *Poiſe your Firelock.*

1ſt Motion.

The ſame as the 1ſt Motion in Explanation 40. tell 1, 2.

2d Motion.

Raiſe the Firelock with the Left Hand, ſeizing with the Right Hand under the Lock; tell 1, 2.

3d Motion.

Thruſt it from you, coming to the Poiſe.

59. *Shoulder your Firelock.*

This is done as in Explanation 26.

LXXXVII

Return your Bayonet.
III.d Motion.

LXXXVIII

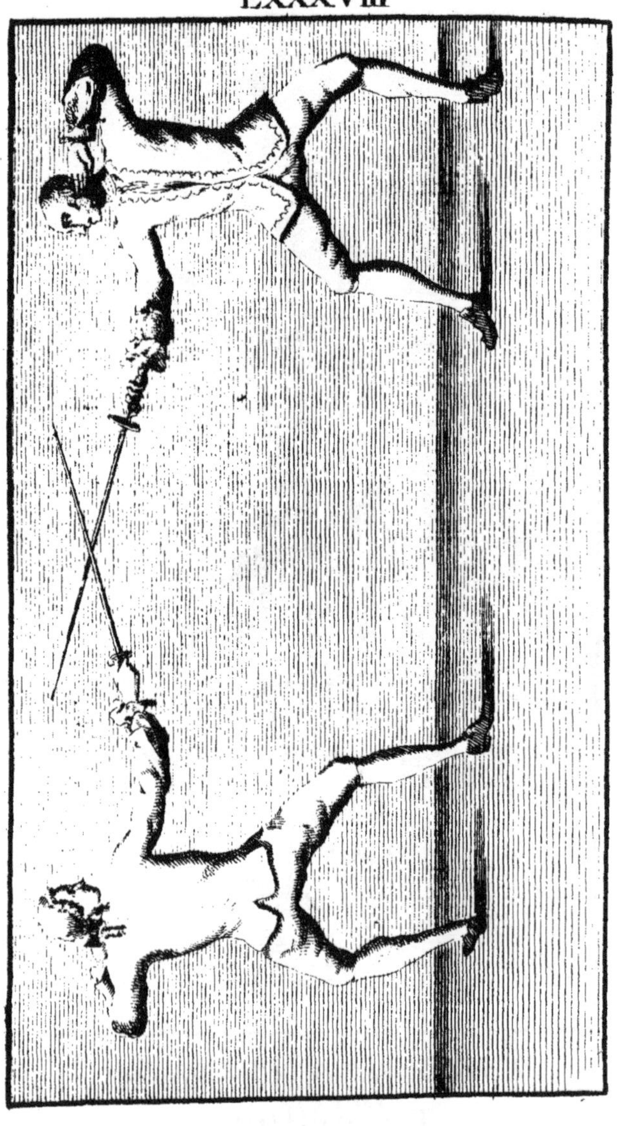

The Guard.

The Sword is to be held, ſteady, and firm, in the Right Hand, upon the Flat or Demy-Carte, with the Nail of the Thumb upwards: The Pummel of the Sword in a Line with the ſhort Ribs; with the Point ſomewhat elevated. The Left Arm elevated, and bent in a Semi-Circle, the Elbow turn'd out; the Left Hand rais'd to the Height of the Left Eye, the Thumb downward; the Shoulders well ſquared, the Body upright, and well edged in a Line, with the Point of your Sword; and which ſhould be ſuſtain'd chiefly on the Left Foot; the Right Foot flat and firm on the Ground; the Right Leg perpendicular; and the Knee a little bent: The Left Toe turn'd outwards, ſo as the Heel may juſt be clear of the Heel of the Right Foot, being diſtant from each other about two Foot: The Head erect, directing your View along the Sword Arm, towards your Enemy.

2. *The Thrust in Carte.*

Having a good Guard as before, and within Meaſure, your Sword engag'd in Carte; you deliver the Thruſt, with a full Longe; dropping the Point, the Nails of the Sword Arm turned upwards; the Wriſt elevated, higher than the Shoulder, and well ſupported with the Arm extended: At the ſame Time throwing off the Left Arm, in a ſtrait Line to the Left, with the Palm upwards; the Body almoſt upright, and well ſupported. The Right Leg perpendicular with the Knee a little bent, the Toe oppoſite to your Adverſary, and in a Line with your Sword. The Left Leg and Thigh extended with a ſtiff Knee, both Feet flat and firm on the Ground; the Head erect and inclining a little over the Right Shoulder, from whence you obſerve your Thruſt.

LXXXIX

XC

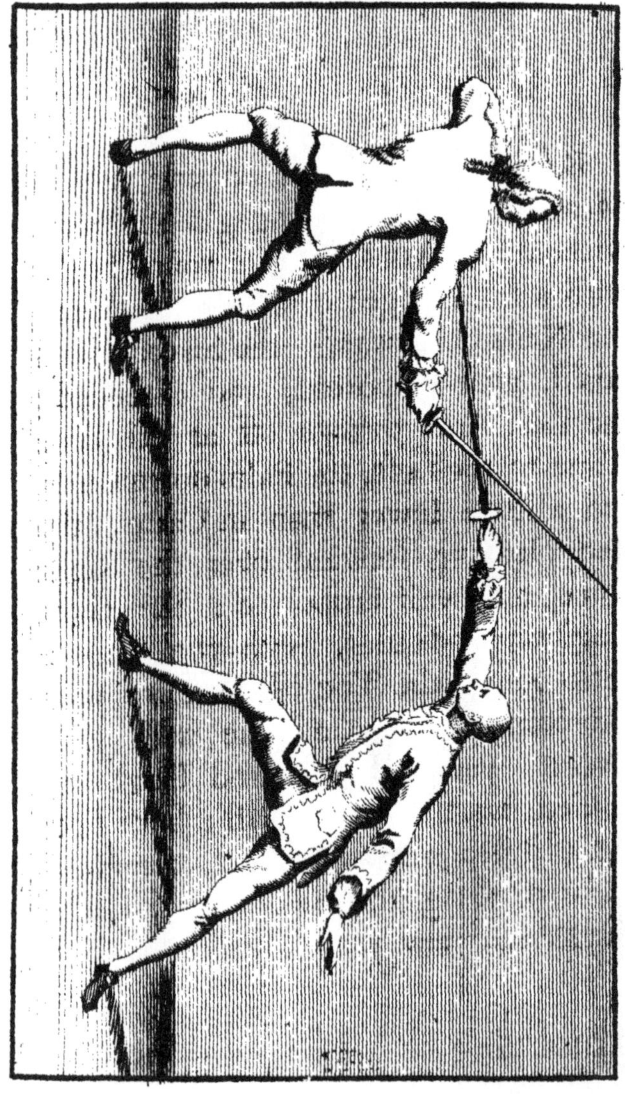

3. *The Thrust in Tierce.*

Being in a good Guard and within Meaſure, the Sword engag'd in Tierce without the Arms, deliver your Thruſt, with a full Longe; dropping the Point; the Nails downwards, the Sword Hand rais'd, well ſupported, and extended; the Left Arm thrown off at the ſame Time to the Left, the Palm downwards, and a little lower than in Carte; the Body leaning forward over the Right Knee, and well ſupported; the Right Leg perpendicular, with the Knee a little bent; the Toe oppoſite to your Adverſary, and in a Line with your Sword; your Left Leg and Thigh extended, with the Knee ſtiff; both Feet flat and firm on the Ground, the Head inclin'd along the Sword Arm, under which you view your Thruſt.

4. *Carte Thruſt under the Arm.*

The Body is in the ſame Attitude, in delivering this Thruſt, as in ſimple Carte; with this Difference, that it is given, under the Adverſaries Sword Arm, which is held too high in Carte.

XCI

XCII

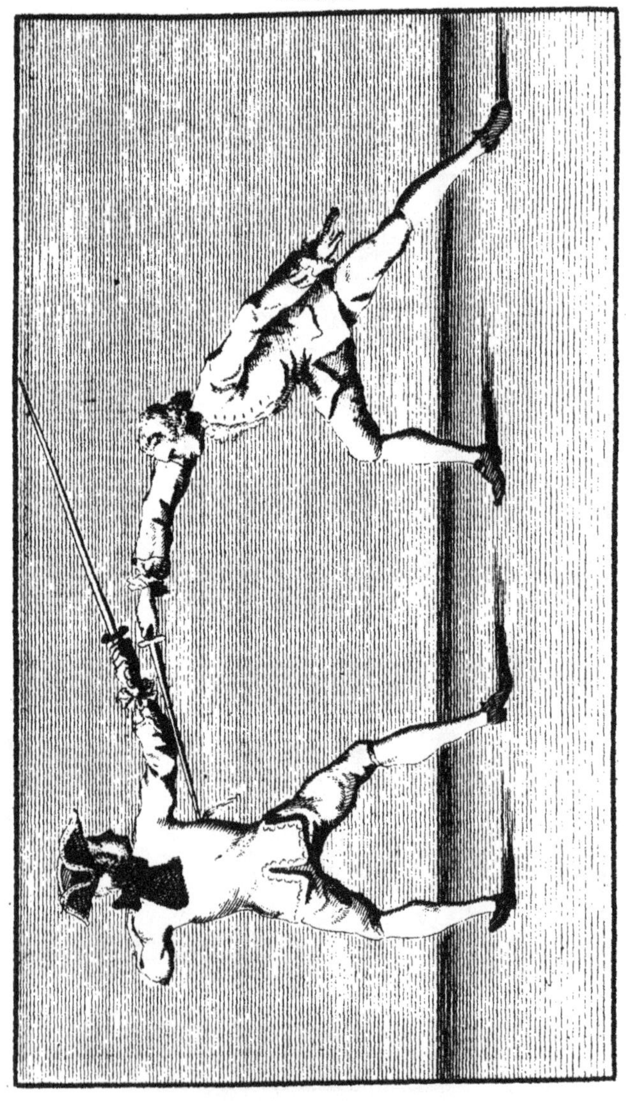

XCI

XCII

5. *The Thruſt in Seconde or Tierce under the Arm.*

This Thruſt is given in the ſame Poſition of Body, as in the high Tierce; only the Adverſaries Sword Arm, being too high in Tierce, it is puſh'd under it.

6. *Tiere thrust on Carte Side.*

This Thruſt is deliver'd, as in the upper Tierce, by reaſon the Enemy holds his Sword in Guard, inclin'd too much to the Right.

XCIII

XCIV

7. *Carte Thruſt over the Arm, or an Outſide Carte.*

This Thruſt is deliver'd in the ſame Poſition of the Body, as in the upper Carte within the Arms; becauſe your Adverſary, holding his Wriſt too low in Tierce, inclines his Point too much to the Left.

8. *The Flanconnade.*

This Thruſt is made, by gaining the Feeble of your Adverſaries Sword, (which may be done without, or upon his Longeing) ſliding forward with the Point directly under your Adverſaries Wriſt, towards his Flank; the Left Hand at the ſame Time brought forward towards the Enemy's Sword; the Poſition of the Body as in Carte.

XCV

XCVI

9. *The Paſs in Tierce.*

Is a Thruſt deliver'd in an outſide upper Tierce, with this Difference, that inſtead of Longeing with the Right Foot you ſtep forward with the Left: The Left Leg is perpendicular whilſt the Right Leg and Thigh are extended; the Toe of the Right Foot on the Ground, and the Heel rais'd.

N. B. *In this Thruſt you double your Velocity, Force and Diſtance.*

www.ingramcontent.com/pod-product-compliance
Lightning Source LLC
Chambersburg PA
CBHW030932150426
42812CB00064B/2821/J

* 9 7 8 1 8 4 7 3 4 3 1 7 8 *